Marketing Jesus' Way

GEORGINA WILSON

Copyright © 2015 Georgina Wilson

All rights reserved

ISBN -10: 1494837463
ISBN-13: 978-1494837464

COPYRIGHT

NKJV - New King James Version ® Copyright © 1982 by Thomas Nelson, Inc

AMP – Amplified Bible Copyright © 1954, 1958, 1962, 1964, 1965, 1987 by The Lockman Foundation

NLT - New Living Translation Copyright © 1996, 2004, 2007 by Tyndale House Foundation

NIV - New International Version ® NIV® Copyright © 1973, 1978, 1984, 2011 by Biblica, Inc ®

All scripture references refer to NKJV unless otherwise stated

DEDICATION

I would like to dedicate this book to God. I thank Him for the revelation and wisdom that He has poured out in me over the years, as without Him I don't know where I would be right now. I have learnt my value, and understood my purpose through our Lord. I am not ashamed to say that I believe that God has equipped me in the area of propelling people into their callings; He allows me to see the vision of what they are yet to give birth to revealing what they are pregnant with. This has been confirmed by a number of fellow Christians and I boast in this not of myself but because it comes from God, He chooses who He blesses and with what. By embracing this I can only attempt to fulfil what our kind, gracious and loving God has destined for me and I cannot achieve this without Him, so thank you Lord for never giving up on me.

CONTENTS

	Acknowledgments	I
1	Setting the foundation	Pg 13
2	God has not forgotten you	Pg 21
3	Creating the right mindset	Pg 28
4	Faith comes by…	Pg 36
5	Marketing – the verb	Pg 47
6	Stay plugged in to your source	Pg 58
7	Give and it will come back	Pg 62
8	Testimonials and referrals	Pg 67
9	Duplicating your resources	Pg 72
10	Plan the way forwards	Pg 76

ACKNOWLEDGMENTS

I would like to acknowledge my brilliant mum Veronica Coghiel. She has been a rock throughout my life, a sister and a friend, I wouldn't be here without you.

Abdul Kamara, thank you for your support and belief in me.

I also thank my Pastors Noel and Sharon Mclean for their vision of raising leaders, and for their commitment and obedience to God; developing and assisting many into their calling and destiny.

PRELUDE

This book is for Christians and non-Christians who have, or would like to start their own business, ministry or charity. It is designed to elaborate on key marketing strategies as seen in the Bible that could help your business excel to great levels.

The first section focuses on how to create the right foundation for you as an individual. The second gives you the marketing strategies to help produce a successful business.

Many of you may have heard, read, and sought advice from many of the great marketing entrepreneurs and experts explaining how we should market our businesses to gain the maximum benefits. I myself have studied many of these teachings and have learnt much along the way. Many of these teaching have made a dramatic difference to how I perceive business and how to go about running a successful business. I have however some to the realisation that Jesus himself was the greatest marketer for the Gospel; He sets us a great example.

It seems funny to view Jesus as a marketing expert. The definition of marketing is "the action or business of promoting and selling products or services". We can all agree that Jesus matched that description not for His own gain but for the gain of mankind.

Follow me as I delve into some of the examples that Jesus set before us which we can use not only in spreading the good news but also in our businesses. Jesus stood up for what He believed in, regardless of what others would say about Him. He made it His objective to make sure that He did everything within His power to show who He was and gave examples of what His purpose was whilst He was here on earth. What an amazing time it was.

"Something I realised some time ago was that my gifts and talents were not given for my benefit"

SECTION 1 – THE GROUNDWORK

CHAPTER 1

SETTING THE FOUNDATION

Firstly I would like to begin with YOU and the journey that has brought you to this point. In Christianity the world of business can be a slippery slope because of all the stipulations attached to being a wealthy Christian. In order to establish more about where you stand I would first ask you this question, why are you going into or why are in the world of business? Stop, pause, have a real think about it and give yourself an honest answer. If your answer is to make lots of money that is great; there would be no real point of going into business if you didn't want to make money. The sole purpose of a business is to be profitable in monetary terms; even charities need to make money to have a vast effect. However if the sole reason for you making lots of money is only for you to purchase that dream house, go on three holidays a year and buy all the clothes you could ever wish for and it stops there, I would have to question whether that is something that you are called to do. As harsh as that may sound, as Christians God gives us the knowledge and the power to gain wealth but it is always related to kingdom building and impacting others in a positive way.

Yes, Christ came that we may have life and enjoy it *(John 10:10)* and there is absolutely nothing wrong in having nice things and living a comfortable wealthy lifestyle. I will even go as far as to say that there is nothing wrong with being a multimillionaire or a billionaire Christian. The whole stigma about having too much wealth as a Christian is wrong; it is not money itself that is evil but the love of money for purely selfish indulgence and self-pleasure that is wrong. This particularly if we fight for it so much that we lose focus on God; this is the route to all evil *(1 Tim 6:10-11)*.

There is always a lot more depth to the gifts we have than to just gratify ourselves. Something I realised some time ago was that the gifts and talents that God gave me were not given only for my benefit; they were not for me to feel proud or good about myself - they were there to help others. If one of my gifts or talents (which all come from God- *James 1:17 NLT)* blesses, sows a seed or has some form or measure in transforming someone else's life, this is where the trueness of these gifts and talents manifest in their given purposes. If our end goal for our business is only to gratify ourselves, I know that this would not be pleasing to God as He asks us to deny ourselves and take up our cross daily *(Luke 9:23)*. We need to seek first the Kingdom of God and His righteousness so that everything – all the things we desire for ourselves can be added *(Matthew 6:31-34 paraphrased)*. The scripture doesn't say seek first everything you need for yourself and then the Kingdom of God. Following this scripture correctly means God gets the glory. Too often we try to get what we want for ourselves without realising that we have a loving Father who cares for us and gives us the desires of hearts *(Psalm 37:4 NLT)* according to His will without us doing a thing. All that He requires is us, and all of us.

Do you believe that you been called into your business? The worst thing you could do is to go into something on your own without God, meaning you have to do all of the work to make it happen. Generally speaking most people will have a measure of understanding about their purpose, which will lead them into what they are called to, it would be their passion and something they are naturally good at. For example, people that are passionate about developing young people tend to be teachers or youth leaders. Maybe you have a real passion for cleaning and start your own cleaning company. Don't be afraid to ask God for clarity; He says ask and it will be given, seek and you will find, knock and the door will be opened *(Luke 11:9)*. Seek God for reassurance in your business or idea. He may give you an immediate answer, or He may say "be still" and reveal more to you at a later date. Just know that His timing is perfect and His word cannot return to Him void. Just keep knocking - it is in His nature to answer you as His child.

If God has called you into something it means there is a divine purpose for it and it is your specific destiny. He will make a way through any circumstance, and no matter what, there is purpose to it. There is nothing greater than knowing that you are in the divine will of God. If He brings you to it He will bring you through it. The emphasis here lies with what He will do and what He is capable of doing. The same God that spoke light into the world has spoken life over you and your business.

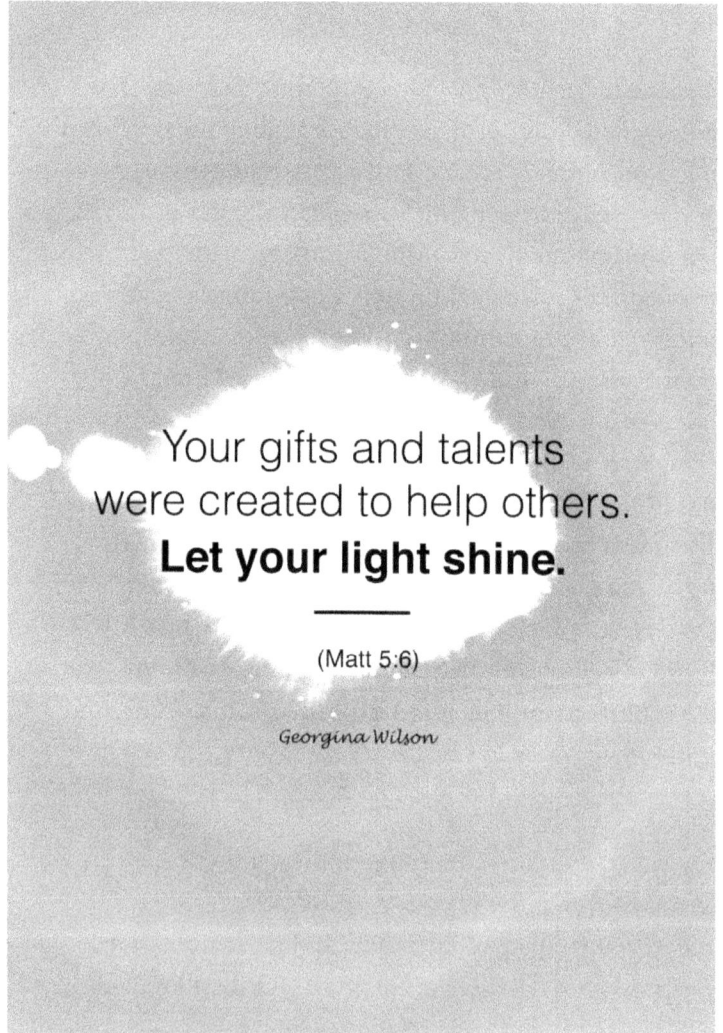

Jesus knew what He was called to do; He said to His parents "I must be about my father's business" *(Luke 2:49)*. There was no mistaking His destiny, Jesus had a deep understanding of what His purpose was and He was determined to achieve what He foreknew.

If you have been called into business, God will make all things possible; all you need to do is to trust in Him. Get out of the boat just as Peter did and keep your eyes on Him.

Matthew 14 (AMP)

[28] And Peter answered Him, Lord, if it is You, command me to come to You on the water.

[29] He said, Come! So Peter got out of the boat and walked on the water, and he came toward Jesus.

[30] But when he perceived *and* felt the strong wind, he was frightened, and as he began to sink, he cried out, Lord, save me [from death]!

[31] Instantly Jesus reached out His hand and caught *and* held him, saying to him, O you of little faith, why did you doubt?

[32] And when they got into the boat, the wind ceased.

Notice that the first thing that Peter did was to ask Jesus to command him to get out of the boat. This re-affirms what we touched on earlier; knowing that God has called you is first and foremost. The next part is actually taking that step of faith just like Peter. I remember in church one day I was saying to God, "I know that you have called me but I have so many areas in my life that I need to improve on before I can really step out. I need to be at a certain level before I think I can, and I've got so much I need to do first". God said to me, "Don't wait until you are perfect to step out. I call you with your imperfections into the unknown where you must rely solely on me and in that place where you have to depend on me, that's where you are transformed."

God knows us so well that He gives us the reassurance to know that even if we take our eyes off Him for a moment and let the things around us change our perception of the miracle that is happening; we can still call on Him and He will rescue us as He did with Peter. God's word says that He takes us out of the pit of destruction, and crowns us with loving kindness *(Psalm 103:4)*. It doesn't matter where you are in your life or business it is not too late - nothing is too difficult for God. *(Jeremiah 32:27 AMP)*

Many of us, especially business people (myself included), have very strong characters and are very sure about what we want and how we want to go about achieving it. I would always set out a plan and make sure that according to that plan I knew all the logistics to how everything would come to pass. So for me I would have had to know that to travel from A to C I would have to go past or through B in order to get there. However God challenged me in this area as He wanted to take control, and likewise He wants to take the driving seat in all of our lives. He took me along many paths where I jumped straight from A to C or in my terms He completely blew everything out of the water, and on many occasions brought me 360 degrees from A to Z in areas of my business. These transitions made no logical sense and had nothing to do with me and my ability. Miracles are birthed by simply saying, "Okay Lord I know this doesn't make any sense in the natural but I know that you are a supernatural God and you know all things, I am going to walk in what you have asked of me". He has never ever failed me to this day! Even when it seems like things will not work out, remember what God declared about you, what your destiny is and believe in your "SUDDENLY" moment *(Isaiah 48:3)*. Once God has called you into business all you need to do is obey His voice and He will do the rest.

Now take a moment to really pray and listen to God and ask him to give you the revelation you need concerning your business, ministry or charity. Ask about the purpose behind this, and begin to set the right foundation.

Once you have done so, write down your unique calling using the lines on the following page. It is well known that writing things down helps us to express what is already within.

Why I am going into or in business?

CHAPTER 2

GOD HAS NOT FORGOTTEN YOU

Are you one of those people that are certain they were called into their business by God? You followed all of the instructions that He gave you but somehow things aren't going according to how you think they should be. In fact you are almost at breaking point, and you are wondering why God called you into this situation. Let me tell you that God has not forgotten you and it is not over yet!

Let's look at Matthew 14:22-27. Jesus instructed His disciples to go into the boat and wait for Him on the other side whilst He sent away the multitudes He had preached to, and fed with the five loaves and fish. But what happened next? Unexpectedly a storm arose, the boat was tossed to and fro and was swept out into the deep sea far away from where they

were meant to be through no fault of their own. Jesus was the one that asked them to wait there.

Can you imagine what they must have been thinking? "Why did Jesus make us wait here knowing what would happen? We are doomed, we don't even know where we are right now, we could die out here, our boat is beginning to fill up with water."

Have you felt that your business has been bruised and battered and tossed to and fro, even though you knew that God called you, and now you are asking, "Where is God? Why has He left me?" Do you know what happened next in the scripture? And let me tell you that the same can apply to your life and business. Just when the disciples were most discouraged and they could not see a way out; when everything seemed to be against them; Jesus walked on water to meet them exactly where they were.

These events allowed them to experience a deeper level of God, they had a revelation of who He was as in *(Matthew 14:33)* saying, "Truly You are the Son of God." They experienced the scripture "I will never leave you nor forsake you" *(Hebrews 13:5).*

Our Lord has not forgotten you. He will meet you wherever you are, even if He needs to walk on water to meet you, He will. Don't give up on what God has asked you to do unless He instructs you otherwise. No matter how weary you become, just as the scripture states "Even young men shall utterly fall and youths shall faint and be weary, but they that wait on the Lord shall renew their strength, they shall mount up with wings as eagles, they shall run and not grow weary, they shall walk and not faint *(Isaiah 40:30-31)*. Wait on the Lord for He will come. Trust in Him and do not look to what is happening around you.

No Matter How bad things look, you are a child of the King

"When you go through rivers of difficulty you shall not drown" Isaiah 43:2 NLT

I myself have always been a very logical person, but when God is ready to transform our lives, logic has nothing to do with it. I have faced situations in business which have seemed impossible to come out of in the natural world. There have been points where I have been at rock bottom; where it took a huge amount of courage to even wake up in the mornings and work. It has taught me a valuable lesson that everything always happens according to God's will and perfect timing.

Sometimes God will say go forward, he may say do this or that or be still; He knows what is right for that season. From my experience trusting that everything would be fine in impossible situations was much easier said than done, especially when it seemed as though there was no hope. My belief that God has a plan, allowed me to live by His grace.

After much turmoil, praying, fasting and seeking God to ask what was happening; I realised that the mistake being made was that God had been taken out of the equation in the business. Both I and my business partner took on the burden of everything ourselves; we were running the business by our own strength and our own means. When we came to the final breaking point we asked the Lord, "You called us into this business. Why is it so hard? Should we close it?" as we felt there was no hope. The Lord then told us that the reason why the business was in its current poor condition was because we were not putting Him first. He said that He instructed and called us into this business and therefore He was the 1st director, we needed to consult Him in everything and understand that we can do nothing without Him. The scripture "Trust in the Lord with all your heart, and lean not on your own understanding; In all your ways acknowledge

Him, and He shall direct your paths." *(Proverbs 3:5-6)* was impressed on our hearts.

We needed to stop taking everything on ourselves and learn to cast our cares and burdens to God because He was able to carry them *(1 Peter 5:7)*. He taught us that as He was part of our business, He had the foresight to see all things and there was a purpose to what we were going through. It was essential to trust Him as He had our best interest at heart. This amazed me and we asked and prayed for God to help us to put Him first in all of our endeavours. I do believe that life changing valuable lessons were learnt during that period, and sometimes you have to learn things the hard way.

God will direct you and if God says it's not over, it is not over. He can turn your ministry and business around in an instance. Wait on the Lord and be of good courage and He will strengthen your heart *(Psalm 27:14)*. After we listened and obeyed, God began to work in ways that made no sense in the business world. He began to open new doors for other opportunities and directed me in these areas, things that I had no experience or qualifications in. Miracles were happening; I was amazed; it was unmerited favour. When I had no hope He restored it to me. I now stand on the knowledge that when I seek the Lord, and the Kingdom of God, and His righteousness, God works behind closed doors and adds everything I need, without me having to do anything. *(Matthew 6:33)*

The funny thing is that I thought that it was all my hard work that would cause my business to do well. In saying that, we must still understand that God does expect us to work, as faith without works is dead *(James 2:20)*, however He has shown me that my success is not based on how great I may think my knowledge is, but based upon Him and how much He decides to bless me. He can move mountains and He can make a way where things seem impossible. He can make 1 + 1 = 5 if He wants and all I need to do is seek Him first before anything and everything. Now that is what I call *awesome*.

If this part of the book reaches out to you I urge you to continue the good fight of faith; put God first in your life and you will see Him work miracles. The race is not given to the swift, but to those who endure to the end *(1 Timothy 6:12, Ecclesiastes 9:11)*.

The Lord promises you in Isaiah 43:2 *(NLT)* that, "When you go through deep waters, I will be with you. When you go through rivers of difficulty, you will not drown. When you walk through the fire of oppression, you will not be burned up; the flames will not consume you". No matter how bad things look you are a child of the King and God has not forgotten you.

Failure is not falling down BUT STAYING DOWN.

Mary Pickford

CHAPTER 3

CREATING THE RIGHT MINDSET

In this section I want to challenge your thought process and take away any limitations set in your mind. Do you think that you are ready to go into business or to take your business to the next level? I hear many say, well yes of course, but I just need to have more time, get a bit more organised, just one more qualification; the list goes on. We have so many excuses as to why we hold back from walking in what God has called us to, and one of the biggest obstacles is ourselves.

It is imperative when you are in the world of business that you have the right mindset. One quote I love is, "if you don't think that you will, then you probably won't". Faith is the "substance of things hoped for, the evidence of things not seen" *(Hebrews 11:1)*. To be successful you must have faith. It states in the Bible that we all have a measure of faith, that faith as small as a mustard seed can move mountains, and with faith nothing is impossible *(Matthew 17:20, Romans 12:3).*

What do you think about yourself? Do you see yourself as being a great achiever in life or do you limit your thinking to mediocrity? In Proverbs 23:7 it tells us, "as a person thinks in his heart so is he" and this gives us the real understanding that we are a replication of our minds thoughts. If you are going into business you must, and I repeat must, think a certain way to aid your success, you must adopt a limitless mindset.

How can we achieve what we need to unless we first believe it in our hearts and minds? In order for us to have a limitless mentality we must have confidence in ourselves and what we can achieve through God. I shared a testimony at one of my Empowering Women in Business sessions which members found really touching; on how I believed in God and had faith in Him and His greatness but, I didn't have enough faith to believe that He could use and work in and though me. I decided that I still wanted to do good and would do as much as I could do myself, until God began to show me that He wanted to use me and revealed how much more I could achieve through Him; that I was good enough not in my own power but because of Him.

There are a number of people with low self-esteem who don't believe that they could ever achieve anything, they have had had failures and have rarely had good outcomes in their lives. Let today be a new day, let us allow ourselves to make the changes that we need to and can do, get practical and utilise the word of God.

Let me also take the time to re-iterate to you that if God has called you into business He has equipped you with everything you need to be successful. He knew exactly what you would face yet He still chose and called you. The fact that you are reading this book is an act of faith in itself.

We see so many examples in the Bible of where God called the most unlikely people to greatness. We can make a choice to accept the calling of being a successful business person or not.

Rev. Michael Beckwith

God asked Moses to lead the children of Israel out of the land of Egypt. It was a great task and he didn't think he was up to it because he had a speech impediment, and so he begged for God not to send him and eventually his brother had to speak on his behalf. Exodus 4 says in the NIV:

[10] Moses said to the LORD, "Pardon your servant, Lord. I have never been eloquent, neither in the past nor since you have spoken to your servant. I am slow of speech and tongue." [11] The LORD said to him, "Who gave human beings their mouths? Who makes them deaf or mute? Who gives them sight or makes them blind? Is it not I, the LORD? [12] Now go; I will help you speak and will teach you what to say."

Do you know that no matter what flaws you may think you have God sees past them. He knows the magnitude of what He has placed in you and your business? How can we question God about who He wants to use and why He wants to use them? He knows all things.

David was merely a shepherd boy yet God called him to be King. He did not complain or look at his faults and weaknesses. It didn't make sense; all of his brothers were much bigger and stronger than him, His father had groomed them in preparation for kingship whilst David just tended the sheep. However he stood and accepted his calling and we see that his boldness and courage came not from himself but from the understanding of how mighty and strong his God was. When Goliath the giant came, David said " Who is this who thinks that he can defile God?"*(1 Samuel 17:26, paraphrased)*. He understood a very good principle; things do not always happen in the way we think they should, but ultimately it is Gods purpose that will reign. Are you standing on our own abilities or are you standing on Gods ability through you. His ability is far beyond anything we could think of? *(Ephesians 3:20)*

What limitations have you put on yourself or what limitations have you allowed others to put on you to stop you from going forward? It is time to "Arise [from the depression and prostration in which circumstances have kept you—rise to a new life]! Shine (be radiant with the glory of the Lord), for your light has come, and the glory of the Lord has risen upon you!" *(Isaiah 60:1 AMP)*. It is time to take a leap of faith, step out of the boat, step out of your comfort zone. Is there anything too difficult for God?

Sometimes we go through situations where our whole world seems to crumble before our eyes it is hard to believe that things can change. Remember if you have faith as small as a mustard seed you can move mountains *(Matthew 17:20 paraphrased)*. Remove the mountain of unbelief in your life and in your business, have faith in the God that called you into your business, trust that He knows what He is doing and take off the limitations. No one is exempt; we all go through things and I have been through some very uncomfortable and unfair situations; sometimes things don't work out, sometimes we get hurt, none of us are perfect, we all make mistakes, but don't let your past rob you from your future. God is able to complete the work that He began in you *(Philippians 1:6)*.

If you can win in your mind YOU ARE MOST OF THE WAY THERE.

Georgina Wilson

People can try put labels on you. If you are not strong enough at the time you might accept what people say, even though this is not what God has said about you. You might see yourself as not being capable of success in business, maybe you believe that this is not for you, or you might try but deep down you have no real high expectations of achieving anything. You may believe that God cannot use you in the area of business because of past mistakes or because of what has been said about you. God says enough is enough. He is capable of doing a new thing in your life so forget the former things; forget the past *(Isaiah 43:18-19)*. Take off the chains of past failures, the heartache, the rejection, the uncertainty and the condemnation, because you are the righteousness of Christ. You can do ALL things through Him; nothing is too difficult. Be the person that God has called you to be with no boundaries or limits attached. Look back on what you wrote as your reasons for going into business and see how much of a blessing your business will be to others.

Press forward in your life, press forward in your business and don't look back. We see what happens in the Bible when we look back though we have been instructed not to. Lot's wife was told not to look back towards Sodom and Gomorrah which God was destroying *(Genesis 19:17 & 26)*; but she did, and subsequently turned into a pillar of salt. It is amazing how we become comfortable to live in unfruitful situations. We can actually miss it when we launch out into newness, even though we know that we are headed to greener pastures. Sometimes we want to look back; but we can only achieve what we need to, by going full steam ahead and keeping our eyes fixed on God; not looking anywhere else but in His direction.

When Moses was leading the children of Israel to the Promised Land they muttered and murmured, "is it not better if we return to Egypt" *(Numbers 14:3)*. Can you believe that they were actually convinced that slavery was better than being free? Some of you reading may be thinking, "maybe I should've just stuck it out with the job I had, at least I knew that I would be getting paid, at least I didn't have this much pressure". God knows the beginning and the end. Let us not be our own hindrances stopping us from reaching and attaining the promises that God has put before us simply because we are still stuck with the "Egypt" mentality like the children of Israel.

God sometimes takes us through some situations that make no sense at all. We must keep our eyes, hearts and minds on Him and He will keep us in perfect peace and never let us go. Others may laugh at you - step out, you may feel crazy - still step out, it may be the hardest thing you have ever done but just keep stepping out!

CHAPTER 4

FAITH COMES BY…

Here we will look into how powerful your words are. In the Bible the power of words is illustrated by God, when He said "Let there be light" it manifested. God says His word cannot return void but it must accomplish that which He pleases and prosper in the thing for which He sent it *(Isaiah 55:11)*.

To develop a mindset that falls in line with our dreams and ambitions, the words we speak must always reflect them. Sometimes we underestimate the importance of this.

The book of Proverbs is a book of knowledge and wisdom written by King Solomon. He was said to be the wisest man in Bible days. One of the scriptures that stood out and made me really think is. "Death and life is in the power of the tongue, and those who love it will eat its fruit" *(Proverbs 18:21)*. Whatever we say has an effect whether it be positive or negative. It produces a seed, either something good or something bad. That seed then produces good or bad fruit. It may sound crazy but try it out and see what happens.

If I ask you this question what would be your answer? Do you want your business to die or to be alive? Hopefully you answered the latter, however what are the words coming out of your mouth relating to yourself and your business. Are you speaking life into it?

Some of the great known motivational and self-help speakers and authors teach methods on how to say the right things about yourself thus changing your mindset. They have taken the word of God and utilised it for their benefit. Some of these principles have been tried, tested and proven to work. Therefore they continue to use them to make progress in their lives and businesses and teach this to others. I wonder how much has been spent on books and seminars to hear information that is actually already in the powerful paperback, hardback or leather bound book called the Bible?

In Matthew 5:25-29 *(AMP)*, there was a woman with the issue of the flow of blood. She had spent every last penny trying to get better but her illness only got worse. She had this sickness for twelve years. Imagine how she must have felt, day in and day out, the same thing and no change. However she did not give up hope and when she heard that Jesus was in town she REPEATEDLY said to herself, "if only I can touch his garment, I will be made whole". There is something very powerful to learn here. Though she had dealt with this sickness for many years and could have lost all hope, whether she knew it or not, she tapped into the great principle about believing and confessing. She set her mind on her healing and believed in her heart that it was possible. She confessed her miracle before it happened. Did she do this firstly to convince herself? We don't know, but we do know that because of her faith the Bible says that she was healed. This form of healing was different; it had not previously been recorded that you could be healed simply by touching Jesus' garment. It was normally based on his own compassion and his reaction, but this woman was prepared to believe in the impossible. Are you prepared to believe that God can do something that seems impossible in your business? Do your thoughts and words go beyond average or what is considered 'the norm'? It couldn't have been easy for her as there were so many people there at the time. She was probably known as the 'sick lady' in the village, and maybe she was embarrassed. There would have been others judging or criticising her for being unclean and trying to touch Jesus but she pushed through what others thought, she pushed through the shame and she pushed through the crowds of people. She finally got the healing that she had been waiting for.

Have you been stuck with the same problems in your business, feelings of hopelessness? Ongoing struggles? I challenge you today to push forward with all that you have; push past your inabilities, push past what others have said about you and take on a new mindset. Decide that you will never be the same again.

The existence of things unseen

Heb 11:1

Faith

Georgina Wilson

So you've read the scriptures and you admire this woman's faith but you still find it difficult to think on a grand scale? Don't worry - that is okay - there are ways to train your mind into thinking BIG. There is a very well known scripture in Romans 10:9 which says 'that if we confess with our mouth and believe in our heart that Jesus is Lord we shall be saved.' We must confess and also believe; that is how we change our mindset. Just as the woman with the issue of the flow of blood believed in her heart but also kept on confessed her healing.

In Jeremiah 14:7 after God told Jeremiah that he was called and created for a specific purpose, Jeremiah said that he was too young. God stopped him in his tracks and said "Do not say that I am too young". He was stopping him from speaking negatively into his destiny. How many times have we done that straight after we have had a great word or clarification regarding our destiny and our businesses?

Do you know who you are? You are fearfully and wonderfully made. God knew you before you were created. You are unique and you are special *(Psalm 139:14, Jeremiah 1:5)*. Your gifts and talents were placed in you before you were born. To take your life and business to the next level, learn how to confess and believe.

The Bible states that we are transformed by the renewing of our mind *(Romans 12:2)*. To be renewed means: to make new, restore, to bring into being again; revive, re-establish *(www.dictionary.com)*. We need to be reprogrammed in our minds using words as a tool to achieve this; faith comes by hearing and hearing the word of God *(Romans 10:17)*.

Let us find some scriptures that can build our faith and change our mindsets. I will note a few faith building scriptures to get you started however you may have some of your own

- I can do ALL things through Christ who strengthens me *(Philippians 4:13)*
- God's grace is sufficient for me *(2 Corinthians 12:9)*
- God has not given me a spirit fear but of POWER and of love and a sound mind. *(2 Timothy 1:7)*
- God has given me the power to get wealth *(Deuteronomy 8:18)*
- He is able to do exceedingly abundantly above all that we could ask or think according to the power that works within us *(Ephesians 3:20)*
- Nothing is too difficult for God *(Jeremiah 32:27, Genesis 18:14)*

I always say if you want something different to happen, you need to do something different in order to achieve it. Write down your five most empowering scriptures on the following page and put either "I" or "me" where it says "us" "you" "we" or any generic terms such as "the World". For example, "For God so loved **me** that He gave His only son so that when **I** believed in Him **I** would not perish but have eternal life. For God did not send his Son into the world to condemn **me**, but so that **I** might be saved through Him" *(John 3:16)*. Do you see how much more real the scripture becomes when you personalise God's purpose for you personally? Even after personalising these scriptures you may still feel unconnected to them, but keep on speaking them into being, call things forth by your words and increase your faith by hearing it; speak life and begin to renew your mind.

Stop Being Negative:

On the flip side, it is also important to stop saying negative things about yourself, business or situation. As I mentioned earlier, how a person thinks in his or her heart so they are. If there is life and death in the power of the tongue; how many times have you killed your own dreams, relationships or businesses simply by opening your mouth? Sometimes we have every excuse as to why everything else caused things to fail but it is time to look in the mirror. Did you say, "I really can't see things picking up", "I can't see us working things out" or "there's no way I can survive in this economy it's just too hard"? I confess that I have been in situations when I have uttered these things. God has had to interrupt me several times to say, "Did I not tell you that you will go through the fire but you won't get burned. Did I not give you the vision for this business and have I not already told you that I will never leave you nor forsake you. I have your best interest at heart" *(Isaiah 43:2 NLT, Hebrews 13:5).*

Yes, we are only human but, if we can apply these principles we can stop the effects of the darts and daggers of our own words from coming to pass. Even when you feel like letting rip do you best to guard your tongue and simply keep your mouth closed. The Bible says "let the weak say I am strong" *(Joel 3:10).* Though it might not be your reality, keep saying it anyway, rather than saying: "I'm so weak". We often hear the saying "mamma always said if you don't have anything nice to say don't say anything at all", which pretty much sums it up.

You have established that this business is your calling; therefore you can stand on the word of God when any negative thoughts come. Just as Jesus overcame the projected thoughts the enemy tried to use to tempt Him in his weakest moments, we need to do the same. For example we hear a thought. "What is the point of all of this? It's too hard". We can counteract this with "let us not grow weary in doing good, for in due season you shall reap if you do not lose heart" (*Galatians 6:9*). We can counteract the thought: "I can't take any more of this", with: "For God will not give you more than you can bear, cast your burdens to Him for his yolk is easy and his burden is light" (*1 Corinthians 10:13 AMP, Matthew 11:28*). In times of financial hardship know that "your God shall supply all of your needs according to His riches in glory" (*Philippians 4:19*).

For every situation there is always something to encourage you in the word of God. What I love about God's promises are that His words cannot return to God void but it shall accomplish all that God set it to do *(Isaiah 55:11 paraphrased)*. It may not always be as quickly as we want it to happen but it is always at the right time according to Gods' purpose for us.

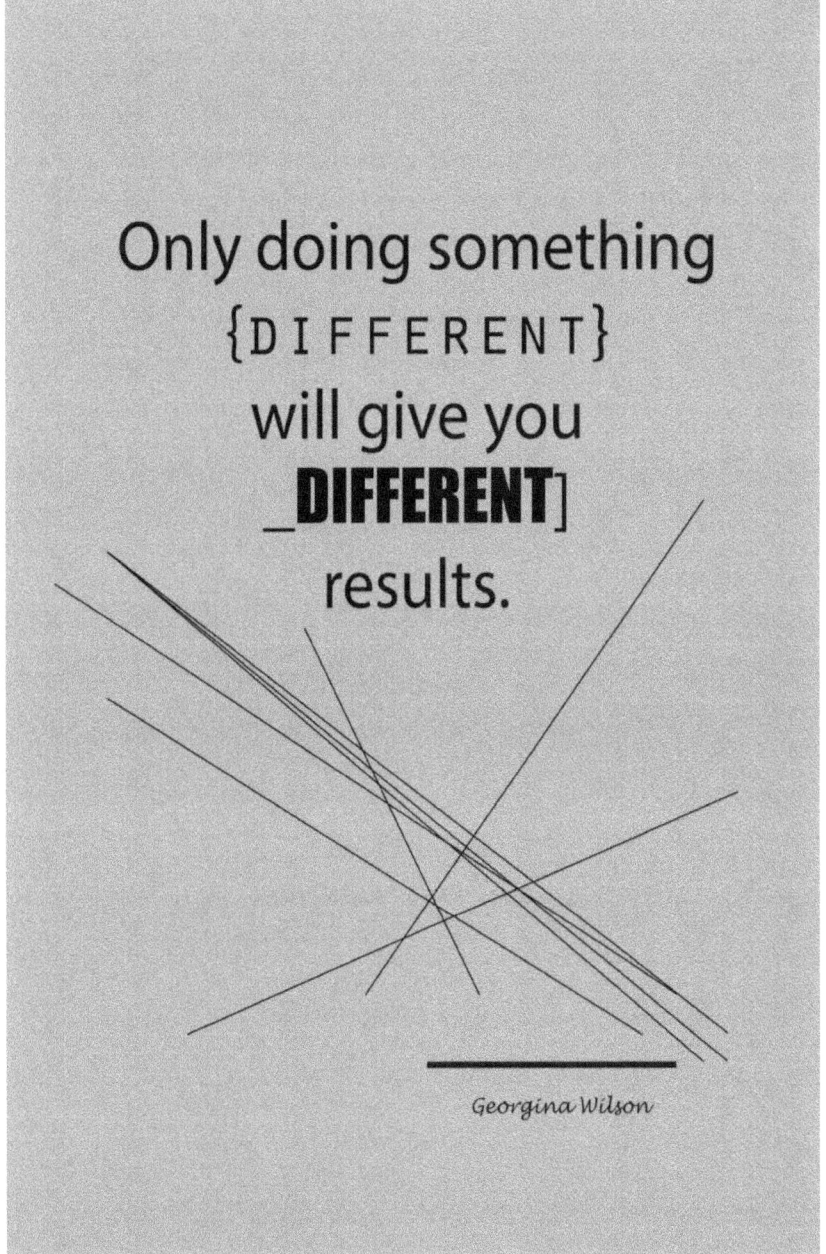

In summary of Section 1 I refer to the book of Habakkuk, which highlights vision, faith, perseverance and truth. You can and will go from strength to strength!

> Habakkuk 2:2-4 The Just Live by Faith
>
> ² Then the LORD answered me and said:
>
> "Write the vision
> And make *it* plain on tablets,
> That he may run who reads it.
> ³ For the vision *is* yet for an appointed time;
> But at the end it will speak, and it will not lie.
> Though it tarries, wait for it;
> Because it will surely come,
> It will not tarry.
>
> ⁴ "Behold the proud,
> His soul is not upright in him;
> But the just shall live by his faith.

SECTION 2 – APPLICATION

CHAPTER 5

MARKETING – THE VERB

Now that we have set the foundation we will now continue by looking into how to use some of the examples proven by Jesus to aid us in our lives and businesses.

Are you currently doing anything in order to promote your business to new and existing customers? Too many of us open a business and then sit inside the shop or office and wait for people to come in, call or place an order. I am a great believer in getting out and making things happen. Jesus went out; He created opportunities to project His message and His purpose. What would have happened if He kept his message to Himself? In Revelation 3:16, God expresses how upsetting it is to Him for someone to be lukewarm. If you have made a decision to be successful at your business you need to give it everything you have. Mediocrity could stop you from being the best, it has to be all or nothing. YOU CAN DO IT! Decide that you will really go for it and give this 110% effort.

Marketing involves the doing verb; taking action, hard work and getting out of your comfort zone. Once we have explored some of these useful strategies we will create an agenda to put them into practice.

If you stay in the same circles and never do anything different how will be able to market your product to new audiences? Getting your business out there can be done in a number of ways, you should have several methods, and at least 8-10 running simultaneously, in order for your business to go to the next level.

Be passionate:

When we think of Jesus and how He went about preaching the Gospel what words spring to mind? Courageous, bold, strong, determined, self-disciplined? He knew exactly what He was here on the earth for and He dedicated his life to this. What business has God called you to? Whatever it may be I reiterate that He has already equipped you with all that you need, however your passion is the fuel that will drive you. Jesus was very well known whilst He was here on earth, why? Because He believed in what He was doing and was not afraid to speak about it to anyone, anywhere. On many occasions He had to quietly disappear from the crowds because they thought that what He was saying was so controversial. *(Luke 4:16-30).*

When we look at some of the biggest entrepreneurs, they have not been afraid to shout about how fantastic their business is, whether others agree or not. What I have learnt is that no one will believe in your product if you do not. If you are not extremely passionate about your business do not expect anyone else to be. Do you talk about what you have to offer to any and everyone? Are you proud to mention it? One of the easiest ways to gain business is through word of mouth and referrals but how will they know if you don't tell them?

> "But how are people to call upon Him Whom they have not believed [in Whom they have no faith, on Whom they have no reliance]? And how are they to believe in Him [adhere to, trust in, and rely upon Him] of Whom they have never heard? And how are they to hear without a preacher?"
>
> *(Romans 10:14 AMP)*

Jesus had an impact everywhere He went. He made it His priority to let people know about the Gospel. Though your business may not have quite as big an impact on someone's life as salvation, I know you have something valuable and of great worth to offer. You may know someone that knows someone that could lead to your best and biggest clients. Nothing is impossible. Be passionate and do not keep quiet about how great your business is!

Target Audience:

First things first; before you decide how you are going to take your business up a notch or many notches, you need to identify your target audience. Is your product or service ideally for men, women or both? What age group does it cater for?

Would it suit middle or working class customers etc? Though the Gospel was for everyone, Jesus had an understanding of who He was sent to reach out to, and who would find it difficult to receive his message. He explains in Matthew 15: 24 "I was not sent except to the lost sheep of the house of Israel." Once you know who your target audience is you can adjust your marketing style to appeal to them specifically.

Website:

I know it may sound strange in today's times but there are a number of businesses without a website. They may be "old school" and think that it is not relevant but I could almost guarantee that they are missing out on business because of this. People looking for products or services nowadays like to do a lot of research beforehand; they like to look at pictures, reviews and testimonials etc. They then make a decision as to whether or not to buy therefore it is imperative that you create a website representing an online version of your office, shop or service. It should be as user friendly as possible and does not need to have bells and whistles but provide enough information to prove that you are an expert and one of the best providers in your field.

You could potentially sell some of your products or services via your website also; so think of it like a sales representative when setting it up or adapting it. Ensure you have some special offers and freebies in order to entice customers, or simply collect their contact details so that you can keep in touch by creating a mailing list. Creating a website does not need to cost you thousands - there are free, easy to use website builders available at my website bizbudee.com. Once created look into search engine optimisation, keywords and pay per click avenues which will help your website rank higher in the search engines such as Google, when customers search for your product or service. If you are not sure of how to do this, educate yourself or find someone that can help through our online business community.

Email Marketing:

Are you keeping their information such as email addresses and telephone numbers? If not, you need to start immediately. Ask them if they would be happy for you to send them special promotions, tips and advice relating to your product or service and create a basic database in Excel, or Word with your customer details.

The good thing about email marketing is that it does not cost you a penny only your time. A key method to being successful at this is to be innovative with what you send. Keep your clients or potential clients updated at least once a month, but preferably every 2-3 weeks with something of value to them. Do not send them anything that is not useful as they will unsubscribe in an instant. For example a hairdresser may send out a mail campaign giving tips on the best hair products to use in hair during summer and at the end of the email offer a 20% discount on those products, if they book a cut and blow dry within 2 weeks. This would be much more enticing to the reader, but if an email was sent titled "Visit my salon" it would not be as inviting for the reader. If this is not your strongest area you can find someone to do these for you at as low as £10.00-£20.00 per email, and it is well worth it. Even if you do not reap the rewards immediately you will remain fresh in your customer's minds, subconsciously this helps them to remember you when they are in need of a product or service you offer or they may refer you to someone else.

It has been proven that the majority of your business will come through re-occurring sales, so rather than only aiming for new customers it is worth reaching out to existing ones. Research says it costs five times as much money for companies to gain a new customer, than it costs to keep an existing one.

Cold Calling:

This is not for the fainthearted but I can safely say that it works. Again if you are finding it difficult personally, please ensure that you find the right people to work along-side you to help. It involves approaching someone that has no knowledge of your business and trying to convert them into a customer. You could say that Jesus did this in His ministry; He stood objectively in front of crowds who had no knowledge of His message and preached the Gospel to them, even though some had not specifically asked for it. This takes boldness and courage. Cold calling either face to face, telephone, or emails can help you to gain new customers. You do however need to target qualified customers and have an understanding of the sales process from start to finish. I do provide this information in some of my workshops.

It is also worth calling your existing customers to follow up on a recent purchase; ask them how they found the product and when they might need it again or see if they would have any other customers to recommend. Make a note of anything relevant and put a reminder in the diary to contact them closer to the time they may need you.

Networking:

It is important to network with others that may need your service or those that can recommend you to others. Research local networking events and visit any that would be of value to you. Speak specifically to those that you could work with, and be clear on exactly how you want to work with them. See how you can help others also and build relationships by doing so. Make sure you follow up once you have left the event as if not it would have all been a waste of time (the most valuable commodity on earth), so use it wisely. Make a note in your diary for when you will follow up which should ideally be no longer than 2-3 days after the event. I have been to several networking events in my time but I find that if you do not prepare and have an objective, you are merely wasting your time. You might as well have stayed at home and watched a film – just saying.

Social Media:

Have you looked at the people sitting at a bus stop, or coffee shop? What do you see everyone doing? The majority are on their smart phones or tablets, more than likely on some form of social media in cyber space. Facebook, Twitter, LinkedIn, Blogs, Google + and YouTube are a few to name, but it is ever evolving. Social media can allow you to gain customers for free and bring exposure to your business. It is important to keep your pages updated on a regular basis at least once or twice a week but for great results daily updates with interesting topics and posts will keep you relevant. If you are not sure on how to go about developing your profiles etc try short courses or hire an expert for a few hours per week. It is definitely a must as it will give your business a real boost, especially when you have lots of followers and activity.

PR (Public Relations):

What is unique about your business or about your story? People buy from people, see how you can be relatable and translate that into something that people would be interested in. For example you might be a mum with twins and you may talk about how you managed having twins and a business at the same time, this could be of interest to some readers who are mothers and they would automatically be more inclined to become customers once they know a bit more about you personally.

Mail Campaigns:

Though mostly everything these days comes in a digital form there are many customers that you could be missing out on who still like to read something in paper form. Reaching out to customers this way does still work and you could even post out something similar to your email campaign for those who still love to hold a glossy piece of paper. The main point is to stay in customers' minds so that they will not forget you.

Stop thinking about all the reasons why you can't and realise why, actually **you can.**

Georgina Wilson

Try, test and try again:

What do you do when you have tried and tried to convince someone how great your business is but they still don't have faith in it?

When Jesus was here He travelled to many different places to inform people about the good news. He also clearly said that He found it very difficult for the people that He knew to accept what He was offering them. I myself love to sing (I am no Mariah Carey!) but I tend to find it much more difficult to sing in front of a crowd that I know rather than to complete strangers. People you know may not believe you are able to own a business; they may believe you are not qualified to offer that service and they might be thinking, "Is this Daniel, Sarah's son who grew up down the road? He's getting a bit too big for his boots isn't he? He must think he is better than us".

You might be lucky enough to have some people close to you that accept you and the business you are developing, however Jesus showed how those closest to Him reacted in Luke 14:30. He also clearly says that when He gave his message and they didn't accept Him He dusted off His feet and went into the next town *(Matthew 10:14)*. I believe that by dusting off His feet and advising the disciples to do the same was a sign of showing that He was not going to let it affect Him going forwards; therefore dusting off any rejection from the lack of acceptance or any affect they could have had. Now I am not saying to just up and leave where you are unless God has instructed you to do so; but you can remove yourself from those that do not accept what you are doing and to prevent their response having an adverse effect on your progress.

If you find that you are at a point where your product or service is not being accepted, don't worry, dust off your feet and try another avenue. Try to reach out to people in a different way. Jesus travelled to places by foot and boat in order to spread the good news but today we have so many other methods that we can use in order to get our business out there to the market.

Don't get hung up on trying to convince someone who doesn't have faith in you or your product as there are plenty of others who will. Keep your head held high and move on.

CHAPTER 6

STAY PLUGGED IN TO YOUR SOURCE

Running a business can be challenging in its own right; doing anything out of the ordinary can have its effect on you. It is important that you stay connected to the "why", the reason you went into business in the first place; i.e. the purpose behind it and why God called you into your business. In the Bible Jesus stayed close to His father; He understood the importance of always going back to His source to help Him to fulfil His destiny. Even when He was completely overwhelmed in the garden of Gethsemane, when the magnitude of what He was about to face came upon Him Jesus went back to His Father and prayed until He felt strong enough to continue His journey *(Matthew 26:36-39)*. We see Jesus quote scripture verses during his time to demonstrate authority and to bring everything under subjection to the word of God. He stood on this authority because He knew what He was talking about and nothing could sway Him. However this level of knowing was not developed overnight. Jesus spent quality, devotional time reading the word of God and communing with His father.

You may have a brilliant revelation about your business and how fantastic it will be, feeling greatly commissioned to go forwards, however it does not end there. You must stay connected to your source. God may want to give you clear directions, He may want to work on your character, He might want to change your mind set. We must make ourselves available to God and spend our closet personal time with Him so that we can continue the race we have begun.

It is extremely important that we put God before our business. In fact I would say that it is detrimental to our success according to His will. It is easy to get caught up in the business, relying on our own strengths and abilities which are nothing compared to what God can do, the easy route is to stay connected. The Bible states that we should not weary to be rich and not to use our own wisdom *(Proverbs 23:4 paraphrased)*. There have been several occasions where I have been so caught up in my business trying to "make things happen" myself. This always seems to be the point where things start falling apart. It is not pretty when God has to get your attention, though He is gracious and faithful. In your schedule which we will create later, include a set time that you will have just to spend with God and read His word so that you can be continually transformed in your everyday life and in your business. Sometimes you might think you do not have the time, but I have learnt (the hard way) that what you try to achieve in three months, God can do in a day if you are close with Him and put Him first.

In our business we had a situation arise that we couldn't understand. We could not get away from it and it kept on haunting us. It was only after we had prayed and then heard from God giving clear instructions that we were to no longer do X or Y that we finally understood what had been causing the problems, and made a decision to do things differently. Sometimes what we think is right, or even what we have good intentions for, if it is not according to God's will or His purpose, will not be fruitful.

> "And you shall remember the Lord your God, for *it is* He who gives you power to get wealth, that He may establish His covenant which He swore to your fathers, as *it is* this day." *(Deuteronomy 8:18)*

We must always remember all that God has done, no matter how successful we become in our businesses.

Secondary to this it is helpful to study and understand your field of business, and to see what is happening with market trends and your industry. Have new things been introduced? Is it something that you could implement? See where things are headed.

Research information from qualified sources via the internet or a book, take up courses, find a mentor who has more experience, buddy up with someone for a week in the field you want to develop to see how they do things. The list is endless but it is important that you take time to develop yourself so that you can be 100% confident.

CHAPTER 7

GIVE AND IT WILL COME BACK

There is one rule that most people believe no matter who they are; give and it will come back to you. There is something deep within us which brings much satisfaction when we give and it is greatly received.

If you look at some of the most successful companies in the world you will notice a similarity to what they have done to build up a huge client base; they have offered something of value, completely free with no obligation. It could be a free product sample, or a free 30 minute consultation etc. Jesus gave on so many different levels and in many different ways. He was the greatest example, and though He gave without expecting anything in return, He did this for a greater reward - to see the lives He touched be transformed. Jesus was moved with compassion and it states in the Bible that the "signs and wonders" were there for the unbelievers, for people that had no initial relationship with Him. He healed the sick, raised the dead, comforted the weak...the list goes on. By doing so He gave a deeper understanding of exactly who God was and demonstrated Gods unreserved free love. The bystanders would see and believe, many of those who themselves had been healed went on to accept Jesus as their Saviour. This is a perfect example of how giving away freely and demonstrating the benefits of what you have to offer can in turn cause your business or ministry to grow.

AOL's (America On-Line) strategy is a typical example of this. Do you remember when almost everyone had AOL on dial up before the wireless internet came about? They gave away 12 months worth of internet completely free knowing there would be an initial period that would cost the company vast amounts of money and the company would be at a loss. However, statistics showed that 80% of the customer consumers would stay with them for an average of 18 months thereafter which would result in record profits. They were the biggest company offering internet and emails for some time before other similar companies emerged.

Sometimes the free product or service offered can have a great impact on a person. They might not be in a position to purchase directly but may be the first to recommend you to others and endorse you. There are many things that you can give away - free products or services, your time or your finances. The Bible clearly states that when you give it will come back to you in abundance, overflowing in fact (*Luke 6:38*). This is something that many business owners have stood by, which has helped them lead to their success.

Tithing *(1 Tenth):*

There are an incredible number of business owners who are not Christians that give 10% of their earnings away every month. Why do they do this? Because they understand the laws of God and they have seen that by giving to charity they cause blessings to flow because God is true to His word.

Now the subject of giving to church can sometimes be a sticky topic, however God looks into our hearts as individuals and it is not based on what the money is used for, God is the judge of that.

I remember when someone said, "I don't know why you are going to church all they want is your money". Many think of a hundred excuses as to why they shouldn't go to church when they don't have the understanding about having a relationship with Christ. My response was, "I am accountable to God formyself. I cannot make myself accountable for anyone else's actions. I do trust that the money goes to a good cause but in the event that there is any misuse I know that God will still bless my tithes and offerings because of my heart".

The subject of giving leads me back to the reason behind your business in Chapter 1. When you set up your business the core reason should go beyond yourself, meaning that the success of your business is determined by its ability to make a difference to others. As mentioned, if you take the focus away from how much you can make for your own gain and set aside your tithes, you will see blessings as a promised by God in Malachi 3:10 AMP:

"Bring all the tithes (the whole tenth of your income) into the storehouse, that there may be food in My house, and prove Me now by it, says the Lord of hosts, if I will not open the windows of heaven for you and pour you out a blessing, that there shall not be room enough to receive it."

Our business is a direct gift from God. He gives us the ability to get wealth. God said we were made in His image and all good things come from God *(Genesis 1:26 & James 1:17)*; therefore all that we have already belongs to Him, and we are merely offering back a portion of what He has given us as a form of gratitude. God sends us even more blessings in return for doing so.

A phrase that I have heard many times is, "you can never out give God" and this is so true, as the more you give the more you receive; this is God's principle. He will always remain true to His word *(Isaiah 55:11)*.

CHAPTER 8

TESTIMONIALS AND REFERRALS

You have product or a service that you want the whole word to see and know how fantastic it is, however it is almost impossible to tell everyone on your own. Research has shown that the easiest way to attract new customers is through testimonials. This is demonstrated in the Bible where we see that Jesus' ministry was enhanced and duplicated through testimonials.

There is a specific story which illustrates this; "the woman at the well" (*John 4:4-30*), where Jesus meets a Samaritan woman on His journey and He requests some water from her at a well. Normally in those days Jews would not associate themselves with Samaritans, so it was strange for Jesus to be by Samaria and to even speak to her. He spoke about her past and present whilst giving her hope by highlighting the living water that would quench her thirst forever. She was amazed at how much Jesus knew about her life, He knew things that she was not proud of, such as the fact that she had been married five times and the person that she was currently with wasn't her husband. I believe personally that she was taken aback by the fact that Jesus sat and spoke with her in His holiness and righteousness and that He offered her this living water freely, despite knowing what life she had lead. Once she had a revelation of who Jesus was she could not contain herself and went into the village and told everyone about what she had experienced, "come see a man!" she said, and the Bible states that many came to Him because of what she said.

This is a great example of how someone having a really good experience with your service or product can have such a great impact on them that it causes them to rave about it. This could result in attracting customers that you might not have been able to reach directly.

Think back to anything new that you have tried or experienced in your life. Was it a recommendation that lead to you trying a new recipe, going to that particular shop, taking your child to that school and so forth? 9 times out of 10 it is the recommendation of others that carries much more weight than anything else. It is received better than any cold call, any advertisement, or any fancy colours or design.

Testimonials and referrals in the business world can be implemented by using a very similar approach used by network marketing companies. This is where you have one person who speaks to two people about the product which they purchased and then those two people speak to another two people and so forth; meaning that the initial person spoken to duplicates into two, four, eight, sixteen, thirty two, etc at a much quicker pace than you would be able to alone. You can potentially reach thousands of people that you would never have been able to reach out to normally. *(Diagram below)*

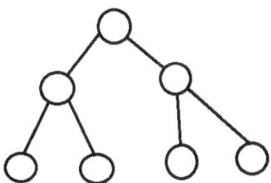

Just in the same way that network marketing offers you a reward for referring other individuals to various products and services, so too can you offer incentives. Some network marketing companies' work well and some are less rewarding but you can utilise these principles to help your business grow. In business one of my mottos is, "if you don't ask you don't get". If you are happy to wait around for everything to happen, you may wait a very long time. Remember Jesus said knock and the door will be opened, seek and you will find. *(Luke 11:9)*

How many clients have you worked with in the past? Most businesses focus on getting new customers but there is much to be done through your existing clients.

If you haven't made some form of database for your existing clients do so as a matter of urgency because as mentioned previously there could be a gold mine waiting there for you. Collate the telephone numbers, email addresses and postal addresses if you have them. Go through your database and ask your clients if they have been satisfied with your product or service. For those that said that "the product was perfect for them", "you've been one of the most helpful companies they used", or "the service was great value for money" etc; explain that you are very pleased that they had such a great experience and ask them if they would be happy to:

a) Allow you share the testimonial. Showcase the testimony on your website, on a business card, in your office, or on social media etc. People love to see what others have experienced in the hope that they will experience the same, even if it is from someone they have never met a testimonial still goes a long way. I know when I go on holiday I always check the reviews others have left on sites such as Trip Adviser and I only make a decision based on the feedback rather than a glitzy website (though the website does have some form of impact).

b) Ask them to recommend a friend or two who they believe would benefit from the service or product. If you feel led you could offer them an incentive for doing so. Most people would be happy to recommend others without any form of incentive once they have received an outstanding service, but by offering them something in return it gives them even more motivation to do so. A good way of doing this is to offer a discount on any repeat business, this way you get to work with them again and show them how fantastic you are a second, third or fourth time around. It is also known that once you have a customer that returns for repeat business they are much more likely to remain with you as their supplier for that service out of loyalty unless something drastic changes, especially when you keep in regular contact with them.

When you contact their referee you can mention the testimonial they gave you, so for example, "Anne recommended you to me hence my email/phone call/letter as she wanted you to have the same great experience working with our company. She specifically said that we were "friendly, helpful and competitively priced", and believes that you would benefit from working with our company. I just wanted to see how we could explore that further".

Imagine you contacted fifty customers, and say 80% of those customers were able to recommend you to two customers each, you would have eighty potential pre qualified customers to contact and convert.

CHAPTER 9

DUPLICATING YOUR RESOURCES

When you are in business, even for myself, one of the hardest things to come to terms with is that it is not possible to do everything yourself. You may be very inspirational, probably the one with all of the product knowledge, you might know all of the services inside out, be the math and accounting whiz, and you are more than likely the one who knows how to make your business brilliant. However there is only one of you! I have said to myself a hundred times, "If only I was an octopus or if only there was three or four of me then I would be able to get everything done, and done the way I want". The reality is that neither is possible.

We learn a really good example of how to be productive by duplicating your knowledge and abilities from Jesus. He was a great and mighty man capable of doing fantastic and magnificent works. However He specifically selected twelve disciples in order to duplicate His works. This helped to continue His message long after He left, the disciples assisted towards the magnitude of the cause. After His commission, Jesus spent much of His time with these disciples to give them understanding, revelation and to empower them with what He had. Though Jesus had much to do, He understood that in order to reach the multitudes, and for His work to continue after He left, He would need to duplicate what He knew. He sent them out two by two to go into the world and preach the Gospel (*Mark 6:7*), enabling the 'Good News' to reach thousands more than He could have on His own. Since then Christianity has become the most widely spread faith throughout the world. If He didn't demonstrate the importance of this I wonder if the Gospel would have reached so many.

We must also take note that Jesus was in close relationship with His disciples; giving them a deeper level or revelation about His purpose and vision. He understood that this impartation was an essential part to His ministry. I believe the disciples were selected based on their individualities, knowing that each would have something different to offer in spreading the good news.

If you have employees select staff members that you feel are willing, skilled and have the ability to capture the vision of where you want the company to go. Make a commitment to spend time with them to teach them specific areas of your business inside out, do this as many times as possible until every aspect of your business is covered. It may be time consuming initially but it has proved very helpful for many of the people I have worked with. A tip is to allow the selected employee to generate a self help manual to cover these aspects of the business, then check through it to ensure that it is all correct. This way a) you know whether the employee has learnt anything, and b) if the employee moves on from the company you have a manual to aid a new employee. Sometimes we think that it is easier to do everything ourselves and create the impossible task of trying to do it all. Take the time out to work with your staff and you will see the rewards.

Some of you reading may not have any staff; which is fine; working with other businesses is also helpful. Find other businesses that could potentially offer your product or service to their clients and offer them a form of commission for doing so; explain your service to them so that they have some measure of understanding for enquiries. This will cost you nothing and payment is only made on results. Confirm what the commission will be, create an agreement and monitor progress; it is a simple as that.

For example a dancing school may speak to acting and music schools and offer a 20% incentive for every new student referred to them that joins their six week program. The acting schools and music schools are incentivised and become motivated to give recommendations to those enquiring about dancing and the dancing school gains new clients. This is a win, win situation which I believe to be a "no brainer".

Make a list on the following page of all the employees you have and what you can teach them, and or the different types of companies that could refer your products or services

… MARKETING JESUS' WAY

CHAPTER 10

PLAN THE WAY FORWARDS

We have covered much, however the most important part is the implementation. We know that faith without works is dead. After reading and evaluating the chapters in this book hopefully you understand what you have been called to and have learnt some vital steps on how to attain this. You should also have some helpful scriptures that you can apply to your life and begin, or continue to have a mind that is being renewed every day. You should now have a clear reason behind why you are doing your business which stems further than just material acquisitions.

We have understood some fantastic marketing strategies to grow our business using some of the examples of how Jesus spread the good news; now we need to make a plan. Luke 6:46-48 explains how we must hear and then take action.

When building a home a good solid foundation is a necessity, which will allow the structure to be strong and solid, as opposed to building a house without a good foundation. When the wind or anything comes against the building it is less likely to stay intact. This is the same in our businesses - set a great foundation for your business so that it is unmovable.

Benjamin Franklin

Let us create a clear mid-term picture of where you want your business to be using What, When, Why and How.

What would you like your business be like in three years (Financially, size of business, number of staff or offices, number of countries etc.)?

When? Timescales involved? (In this case we are using three years, but feel free to adapt as you wish)

Why are you trying to achieve this? What will be the impact both for you and others?

How? What things will you implement to make this happen? Be specific.

One good saying I love is, "if you don't know where you are going, how do you expect to get there?"

In Habakkuk it states, "Write the vision in plain English" (*2:2-3*). Doing this is incredible as every time you see this and read it you can be extremely encouraged and strengthened. It confirms your purpose, capability, what you are going to achieve and it also keeps you in check.

Remember the vision we discussed and what you wrote in chapter 1 regarding why you have, or want to go into business. Write out your vision plain and simple incorporating this, the empowering personalised scriptures you wrote in chapter 4 with your what, why when and how reasons as above (you can use my example on the following page as a reference). Once completed place this somewhere that you go past on a regular basis such as the bathroom, bedroom or maybe on your desktop. Make a commitment to read it every day at least twice a day. There is something very powerful about doing this, as we have learnt; it begins to transform your mindset so even though you may not be there yet, though it may seem to be taking a while, you still know where you are headed. It ignites your faith, the hope for things that are currently nonexistent. Also confess it out loud, you may feel a little crazy but we know what a magnificent impact this will have on your life and in your business so what is the harm in trying?

Example - Jonathan's 3 year plan

"I, Jonathan, can do all things through Christ who strengthens me. I am a mighty man of valour. I have a plan for my life, a future and a hope. I have the knowledge and the power to get wealth. My God can do exceedingly and abundantly above all that could I ask or think. Within the next 3 years I will be a successful businessman and own 2 top class restaurants in the city of London. By year 3 my income after tax will exceed £150,000 per year. I will extend my gifts and talents to those in need, and create a pilot scheme where I will go into prisons to teach men how to be chefs and offer them the opportunity to work in my 3rd restaurant. I will support soup kitchens where the homeless can come for food, and I will begin to save towards opening one of my own soup kitchens where those that are in need can receive nourishing food as well as the opportunity to hear about the Gospel of Christ. I will live a joyful comfortable life with everything I need and more, and I will walk in the purpose that I was destined for. I will achieve this by creating a clear plan and being disciplined enough to follow it, I will step out and be bold, and building a team of senior staff who are dedicated to their work. Nothing is impossible with God."

Take some time out now to write a draft of your 3 year vision.

Date: _____

Vision: _____
_____
_____
_____
_____
_____
_____
_____
_____
_____
_____
_____
_____
_____
_____
_____
_____
_____
_____
_____
_____
_____

Now that you have created your personal statement for the next three years you can create a collage with pictures to go next to it in order to visualise this becoming a reality. Put up pictures of your dream car, holiday destination, perfect home, and pictures of those you want to reach out to etc. In Jonathan's case he could find pictures of great food, fantastic looking restaurants, prison inmates cooking, people waiting in a line for food, etc. You can find almost any pictures required on the internet, some for free; creating a visual version adding even more of an impact.

Creating a Weekly Planner:

To be successful in business you need to be successful in your personal life also - there must always be balance. When planning your timetable you must include the following:

Family: Marriage/ partner, children, date nights, family outings, fun time at home, future planning etc

Faith: church / meetings, prayer and devotional time, reading, Bible studies etc

Personal Time: retreats, gym, hobbies, meeting friends, personal development etc

Business/Work: Marketing, planning, production, meetings, staff development etc.

It may seem like a lot to do but if you implement these points into a timetable format I am almost certain that it will cause you and your business to progress. Now let's create a clear schedule to include all of the points raised. You will still have your normal business duties to carry out as per usual such as answering the phone and actually delivering your product if these are your duties, but by adding in this marketing schedule alongside other mandatory tasks such as bookkeeping and staff reviews, it will help your business to be more successful.

By creating three hour slots you can set yourself a clear plan and schedule to follow. Again this can be placed somewhere for you to see on a regular basis. Try to be as specific as possible so that everything has its place. The key here is to be disciplined enough to follow it as without the fruit of self – control it will all be in vain.

You can make things clearer by writing in different colours to indicate the different areas of Business, Faith, and Family Personal.

You might only have highlighted a few slots specific to faith, however I do believe that keeping God central and by acknowledging God in everything we do and every step we take that "it will be well with us" as in *Proverbs 3:5-6*.

Your chart may vary in many different ways. You might be in full time work and have to work on your business in the evenings and weekends, you may work part-time, or you might need to complete a chart for week one and then another for week two as it varies. You will know how your chart should look, and if in doubt pray, but try to ensure that everything has its place.

Incorporate some specifics within the slots so that there is a form of structure in place. For example you may know that Friday afternoons are quiet and would be a perfect time to do bookkeeping, write this into your schedule also.

See my example for guidance for a mother of two children who is working on her own business part-time on the following page.

Your GIFT is YOUR calling.

Weekly Planner

GEORGINA WILSON

	9am-12pm	12pm-3pm	3pm-6pm	6pm-9pm
Monday	Set Weekly Targets Social Media Marketing Call 10 existing Clients	Gather info for email marketing send out campaign	Family Time – Reading Homework, Dinner Prep	Devotional Reading Family Review
Tuesday	Find 5 Referrals	PR Campaigns, Blogs	Family Time - Reading Homework, Dinner Prep	Gym, meet with friends
Wednesday	Business Network Breakfast Social Media Marketing	Email 10 new customers Staff Reviews	Family Time - Reading Homework, Dinner Prep	Bible Studies
Thursday	Work on Freebies	Search Engine Optimisation	Family Time – Reading Homework, Dinner Prep	Gym, Networking
Friday	Call 10 new customers	Bookkeeping, Weekly Business Review	Family Time - Reading Homework, Dinner Prep	Date Night
Saturday	Housework, Shopping Gym	Family Fun	Family Fun	Family Fun
Sunday	Morning Prayers / Church	Church	Family time	Reading and Personal Development

MARKETING JESUS' WAY

Weekly Planner

	9am-12pm	12pm-3pm	3pm-6pm	6pm-9pm
Monday				
Tuesday				
Wednesday				
Thursday				
Friday				
Saturday				
Sunday				

Of course life is not as straight forward as creating a schedule and sticking to it as things happen but by having it there in black and white, or colours, it brings your attention to a set regime. Therefore if you haven't been able to complete a particular task at the designated time, you will subconsciously know that it still needs to be done and re-schedule time to do it if you have overspent time in another area.

The main thing to remember to make time for everything and try not to neglect any particular area as things can begin malfunctioning if you do not spend any time working on it. Remember to seek God first and His plan for our lives, and His righteousness.

SUMMARY

Here is a quick recap of the main points learnt

- Your business is beyond you
- Renew your mind and change your thinking
- Be passionate and believe in yourself
- Think about what you can give away for free
- Put several marketing strategies into place
  - ✓ Website and PPC
  - ✓ Social Media
  - ✓ Emails
  - ✓ Cold Calling
  - ✓ Networking
  - ✓ Referrals and duplication
- Stay close to your source
- Write your vision and create a timetable – read daily

Now with everything you have learnt go and be the best you that you can be according to Gods calling on your life. I wait to hear about your success!

ABOUT THE AUTHOR

I have been in the world of business for over 14 years ranging from Personalised Products to Property where we help novice investors to learn the secrets about making money from property. I also own a community coffee shop in South London where we not only serve delicious teas, coffees, cakes and desserts but also host a range of events including open mic nights, family fun days, art exhibitions and more. I am a qualified mentor and public speaker with a real passion to see businesses grow and succeed. My latest website **www.bizbudee.com** has been set up as a great tool to help businesses work and grow together helping small businesses to grow with free membership. Throughout the process of business I have had great successes, and on the other hand have had much to learn from. I have a young daughter who is the love of my life and is totally full of character (I have no idea where she gets it from). By no means am I perfect, and in all of my experiences I have come to an understanding that I can do nothing without God, and so I continue to put my faith in Him as my ever present help.

MARKETING JESUS' WAY

www.ingramcontent.com/pod-product-compliance
Lightning Source LLC
Chambersburg PA
CBHW051814170526
45167CB00005B/2012